Scary Fast Launch Assist

Thunderbox Digital

ALSO BY BRIAN MICHAEL STEGNER

SCARY FAST
Scary Fast: The 400% Principle (coming 2023)*
Scary Fast
Scary Fast: Launch Assist

CRUNCHY DUNGEON
Exploring the Crunchy Dungeon (coming 2023)*
A Husband's Survival Guide to the Crunchy Life
Life with a Crunchy Wife - Volume 1
Life with a Crunchy Wife - Volume 2
Life with a Crunchy Wife - Volume 3

THE ADVENTURES OF JOME
The Assorted Adventures of Jome (coming 2023)*
The First Adventures of Jome
The Original Adventures of Jome
The Next Adventures of Jome
The Mysterious Adventures of Jome

VOICES IN THE VOID
VV0.5 (coming 2023)*
Voices in the Void
Voices in the Void II (coming 2023)

FAMILY LIFE
Skipping Adolescence
Skipping Adolescence Workbook

CHRISTIAN MINISTRY
One Thousand Churches

AUTOBIOGRAPHICAL
Europe is Mostly Empty (coming 2023)

*Indicates series introduction, available exclusively on Amazon Kindle for just 99 cents.

Join the BMS Mailing List for promos & free content, visit BrianMichaelStegner.com

SCARY FAST LAUNCH ASSIST

9 Weeks of Practical Guidance to Help You Go Faster

BRIAN MICHAEL STEGNER

Published by Thunderbox Digital
CP80030 Principale
Chateauguay, QC J6J 5X2
Canada

First Print Edition - 2023 v1.2

© 2023 Brian Michael Stegner. All rights reserved. No portion of this book may be reproduced in any form without permission from the publisher, except as permitted by U.S. copyright law. For permissions contact:

permissions@thunderboxdigitial.com

ISBN: 9798372011304

Visit the author's website at BrianMichaelStegner.com

Author Photo by Jess Bernier Photography

Dedicated to everyone who loved "Scary Fast" but wanted more.

Soli Deo gloria

Contents

Introduction	VII
Week 1	3
Week 2	13
Week 3	23
Week 4	33
Week 5	43
Week 6	53
Week 7	63
Week 8	73
Week 9	83
Conclusion	91

Introduction

WELCOME!

You're probably reading this because on some level you're looking at your life and thinking, "I wish I was able to get *more* done, or at least get stuff done *faster*." And perhaps despite great intentions, you often find yourself lying facedown on your couch, unable to reach your phone, struggling to will yourself to get up and just get started (see cover of book).

If that's you, you're in the right place.

You can think of this book as a sort of "Couch to 5K" guide to being more productive (but with no running). It's designed to gently launch you into a more productive lifestyle. Baby-steps toward being faster, all the way up to being *Scary* Fast.

| ABOUT THIS GUIDE

Launch Assist is organized by *week* and by *day*.

Each week has a *theme* and each day involves tackling a small *win*, or *hack* that fits within that larger theme. Subsequent wins and hacks are often logically or practically stacked upon those that have come prior.

Some wins and hacks are labeled as *repeatable* and are meant to be cumulative. In other words, if it makes sense for you to do this new XYZ thing on a daily basis for the rest of your life, then seek to add that small win into your permanent routine.

Just how repeatable it is may vary, meaning it could be repeatable on a daily, weekly, monthly, or even annual basis. Each variation will be clearly labeled.

Other weeks involve a theme with a goal that is *cumulative*, meaning it probably can't be accomplished in a single day. For those weeks each day will involve a *step*. Steps may lead to the completion of a goal within that same week, or might represent an ongoing process that takes longer. Either outcome is OK.

| ADDITIONAL NOTES

If following through on a particular week proves difficult, it's OK to do that week over again before moving on to the next week.

Ideally, plan ahead to tackle these nine weeks all in a row at a time when you're not going to be traveling or going through an unusual life change (moving houses, getting married, etc.). You can, however, intentionally build in an "anticipated" pause if it is of a limited duration (no more than a week or two at most). And if you do take a planned break, you should still seek to maintain as many of the repeatable accumulated wins as you've already started.

Some days will feature "bonus wins" which are additional items that you might find useful to employ, if they apply to you.

As you get further along you'll find less wins and more hacks. Again "wins" & "hacks" may be stackable and should be repeated as directed, when possible.

If by the end of these nine weeks you feel ready for *more* speed, you can safely jump right into reading the original Scary Fast book and study the advanced hacks. Learn more at ScaryFastBook.com

Happy Launching!

Discipline creates lifestyle.

- Hal Elrod

Week 1

Mastering Mornings

This week we're going to focus on mastering the first few minutes of the day.

Everything else builds on getting this right.

| MONDAY

Win: Get Out Of Bed Immediately

Repeat: Daily

Mastering your morning starts the moment the alarm rings, the moment consciousness replaces your dream state, the moment you start making *choices*. Get out of bed immediately: no hitting snooze, no looking at your phone.

Some folks talk about getting out on "the wrong side of the bed" and how that causes them to experience a negative emotional state throughout the whole day, presuming that they're going to be able to "reset" during the next night's sleep and have a fresh start the following morning.

True or not physiologically, this does hold true for your productivity. It's within those first few moments each morning that you decide if you're going to attack the day and wrestle it into submission or if you're going to let it pile up and crush the life out of you.

Hitting snooze, even once, puts you on the defensive.[1] Attacking the day without an early morning compromise or concession puts you on the offensive and is the very first step toward having a productive day. Get out of bed immediately.

---

1. Check out "The Miracle Morning" by Hal Elrod

| TUESDAY

Win: Make Your Bed

Repeat: Daily

There are whole books written on this subject, but all you really need to keep in mind is that after you've decided to take action by actually getting up and out of bed right away, the very next compromise waiting to trip you up is to leave your bed unmade. Win-stacking is a huge part of building up productivity-momentum, and making your bed is the first "next-layer" in that stack.

YOU: "What about the other person who is still in my bed?"

That's a great point. No one wants the sheet pulled up over their face like they've died. Nor do they want to be woken up by overly energetic bed-making, so what I recommend is quietly and gently make *your* half of the bed. It can be as simple as pulling the layers smooth and arranging the pillow(s). And there is an excellent chance that they'll do *their* half after waking and seeing it 50% already accomplished, and you'll gain the secondary effect of being greeted by a made bed in the evening (this carries more psychological weight than you'd imagine). Make your bed.[2]

---

2. Check out "Make Your Bed" by Admiral William H. McRaven

| WEDNESDAY

Win: Brush & Floss Your Teeth

Repeat: Daily

Not only will this help you wake up, it will help shift your mindset into go-mode. This happens for a few reasons: One, it is a proven fact that dressing up changes your mental state (the same way as a million other things, such as body posture, smiling, etc.). Brushing your teeth is like putting your mouth into business-class attire. Two, having a socially-ready mouth (breath, teeth, etc.) removes a psychological barrier that is sometimes present (consciously or unconsciously). This gets us into a "ready-state" to engage with people. On top of that, the biggest win here is flossing. Flossing as a concept represents a huge area of *guilt* and *failure*. Everyone knows they're supposed to do it, but almost no one does. <u>It is a *totem* of our collective failure as a society</u>. But be that person who flosses every morning and suddenly you're crushing it! (The bar on oral care is really that low.) Side-Note: apparently *not* flossing increases inflammation in your body equal to a 10 x 10 cm wound on your chest (according to my dentist), moreover some studies suggest gingivitis may be a cause of Alzheimer's disease[3]. Brush & floss your teeth.

---

3. https://www.alzheimers.net/alzheimers-and-gingivitis-disease-linked-to-gum-disease

| THURSDAY

Win: Drink Some Water

Repeat: Daily

North American "failure totem" #2 is drinking enough water. For sure, some folks drink *too much* water and deplete their salts, but most people aren't drinking enough, and aren't starting soon enough. You know the stats, our bodies are mostly made up of water, and that water needs to be replaced. Add fresh water into your body first thing in the morning. Get it from a good water source (a reverse osmosis set up under the kitchen sink or Berkey filter is probably a wise investment). You don't have to drink a lot, but just enough to get that extra blood circulating into new areas as you stimulate your digestive system. You can put a grain of Himalayan or Celtic salt on your tongue first to open your cell walls to allow for maximal water absorption.[4] This will help prevent having to go to the bathroom one hundred million times. Starting with water also helps guard against the temptation to drink coffee immediately, which isn't horrible, but perhaps isn't the very first thing you should be dropping into your system to start off each day.

Drink some water.

---

4. https://youtu.be/cBuK73K7t_0

| FRIDAY

Win: Do Some Push-Ups

Repeat: Daily

Once you've gotten up, made your bed, brushed & flossed, drank some water, now you're ready to do some push-ups.

YOU: "I can't do any push-ups."

And you think that this means you shouldn't try and do any?...wouldn't the opposite be true? If you can't do any then that's an excellent reason to start trying.

If you've never done a push-up, lay face down on the floor with your feet at a right angle to your body so you can lift yourself up on your toes (it's helpful if you're not wearing socks). Put your palms on the floor right next to your body just below your shoulders, tucking your arms & elbows in. Then "push-up" until your arms are straight. If you can't do it, drop your knees to the floor and use them as contact points instead of your toes.

Do this daily until you're able to do 10-30 push-ups. This will further wake up & activate your body, as well as release testosterone into your system, which is a critical productivity hormone (for both men & women).

Do some push-ups.

| SATURDAY

Win: Get Dressed

Repeat: Daily

YOU: "But it's Saturday!"

Yes, I did this on purpose, supposing that perhaps getting dressed wasn't optional mid-week. But now we're into the weekend and you thought that it might be OK to stay in your PJ's a little longer. And yes there's nothing wrong with that, under normal circumstances. But for this current project, make it a daily win to get dressed every day. Once you've mastered all things productivity, you can cut yourself some slack and have a "cheat" day on the weekend where you don't do any of this stuff, but I wouldn't recommend that at this point. Like we talked about before with "dressing up your mouth" by brushing your teeth, you want to actually get dressed for your day for the effect on your mind. Obviously tailor your outfit to what you have planned (exercising, gardening, shopping, etc.) but if you have flexibility in your choice, I recommend getting a little bit more dressed up than you normally would. So like, maybe not the yoga pants and hoodie, wear <u>actual</u> pants. **BONUS:** If you are showering, end your shower with thirty seconds of cool water (if you can safely do this, consult your health care practitioner if unsure).

Get dressed.

| SUNDAY

Win: Eat Some Protein

Repeat: Daily

Finish waking up your body by eating. So many people don't eat breakfast, even though supposedly "it's the most important meal of the day" (failure totem #3?). You don't have to make it a huge meal, just 10-20 grams of protein within the first half hour of waking will do it. I prefer a natural protein shake and a bit of coffee (after water) to start my day. By starting with protein you're giving your body the signal that you'd like to build muscle today, reinforcing what those push-ups were saying to your body a few minutes ago. I know it's not probably accurate but I think of food in four broad categories, each with a natural long-term outcome:

Protein = Muscle

Carbohydrates = Fat

Sugar = Pro-Cancer (and more fat)

Fruits & Vegetable = Anti-Cancer

Again, probably not entirely true but perhaps a helpful rule of thumb when making food-choices (who doesn't want to be ripped and cancer-free?).

Eat some protein.

Lost time is never found again.

- Benjamin Franklin

Week 2

Rescuing Time

YOU: "Alright, what new stuff are we going to do this week?"

ME: "Nothing."

YOU: "What?"

Before we focus on doing any more *new stuff*, we're going to work on reclaiming some time back from activities that you don't need to be doing.

| MONDAY

Win: Cut Your Social Media Consumption in Half

Repeat: Daily

From this point forward, cut your social media use by 50%. This is as opposed to going cold-turkey and removing it from your life entirely, which might be something you want to consider, but given that so many people use it to stay connected with family, informed on the doings of their social circle, for events and news and everything else, the goal isn't to remove it completely. Instead it's to cut out the endless doom-scrolling that the apps are designed to cause you to do. You've long finished reading what you *meant* to read and even what you actually *want* to read, but you can't help but keep scrolling a little longer, a little more, and it ends up eating up at least <u>twice</u> as much time as necessary. Look in your phone's app-tracking usage functions (or download an app that'll track that stuff for you if your phone doesn't provide it natively) and take what you find and cut it in half. Then use either native or third-party time-blocking settings to limit how long you can scroll before the app shuts down. Get technical assistance with this if you're out of your depth.

Cut your social media consumption in half.

BONUS WIN: Remove all video apps (Netflix, YouTube, etc.) from your smartphone completely.

| TUESDAY

Win: Batch Your Email Work

Repeat: Daily

Repeatedly checking your email is a hidden time-killer. Unlike social media, you *feel* like you're doing something important, but just like social media, the reason you're checking your email is for the dopamine hit that you're mildly dependent on. Need a pick-me-up? Just imagine what might be in your inbox. Boom. Just before you actually look, you're receiving a small hit of drugs in your system. So you do this way, way more times than you need to, and justify it because it's "work-related." But instead, what's really happening is you've now been distracted from whatever else you were supposed to be doing, and you'll waste precious minutes refocusing, over and over again. No one really needs an email reply within a few minutes or they would just text or call.

Instead, set fixed times that you're going to check your inboxes, and no more than four times a day. If that's too hard, start with six times a day and work your way down to four over the course of this week.

Batch your email work.

BONUS WIN: Batch your social media consumption (already reduced to 50% in duration) to a single daily check-in.

| WEDNESDAY

Win: Redeem Your Commute

Repeat: Daily (On Work-Days)

Even if your commute is only thirty minutes, there & back five days a week is FIVE HOURS of time. You will find no larger block of time in your life that you can so quickly put to work for you. And many people have commutes that are at least twice that, equal to more than a full working day each week. If only you had one extra day a week to invest in X, Y, Z, right? Well there it is, claim it.

Now if you drive yourself that obviously limits greatly what you can do (unless you own a self-driving car, which is a thing now I guess). I would think in terms of continuing education, listening to classes or audio books or podcasts is an option. Work on learning that foreign language you want (or need) to learn. Take business classes by audiobook, etc.

But if you take public transport that allows for a WiFi or cell signal, you can use that time to check your calendar, clear your inboxes, plan your day, spiritual disciplines, etc. <u>Don't</u> spend that time on social media or playing games, use it to get a jump on your day.

Redeem your commute.

| THURSDAY

Win: No Phone in the Bathroom

Repeat: Daily

YOU: "But this is like redeeming my commute, I'm just making good use of the time, redeeming my *commode*!"

No you aren't, you're making what should be a 2-3 minute trip to the bathroom into a 5-10 minute scroll-fest. All of those extra minutes add up, and there are unfortunate medical side effects from sitting too long on a toilet seat, you don't need that in your life.

YOU: "So what, I just leave my phone behind when I go?"

Yep. If you're at home this is easy. Or if you're out in public then you'll have to just leave it in your purse or pocket. Use self-control.

Be prepared for this to be a hard one. The habit will be strong. You might want / need to have a transitional replacement habit, a small object you can fiddle with instead of your phone, such as a pack of cards. The hand-feel will be similar and ease the cravings. People might think you have a gambling problem but that's the cost of being more productive.

No phone in the bathroom.

| FRIDAY

Win: Isolate Yourself

Repeat: As Necessary

One of the big time-sucks that you don't have quite as much control over is interacting with other people. Real human interaction time is very important and valuable for so many reasons, but also incredibly costly. I'm not suggesting you become some kind of productivity hermit, but you should attempt to evaluate if there are any situations or even relationships in your life that are taking up more time than they should. This could be the location of where you've chosen to work, such as a high-traffic area with a lot of casual interruptions. Moving to a more physically isolated spot reduces casual interruptions and even "hides" you from those who might try to interrupt out of their own need for distraction. Remember that every interruption requires a refocusing period, meaning when someone "only needs five minutes" you're really giving up 10-15 minutes because they have underestimated how long it'll take AND you're going to need at least five minutes to re-engage with your task. Four "only five minutes" requests a day is actually an hour of lost time. Headphones are a great social barrier to signal to people that you're focusing & unavailable, and set your phone to "do not disturb" if possible.

Isolate yourself.

| SATURDAY

Hack: Merge Tasks

Repeat: As Possible

YOU: "What does that even mean?"

I'll get to that, but first a quick word on "hacks" as this is our first one so far. As opposed to "wins" which are more focused on overcoming specific challenges, hacks are more like tricks that should enable you to be more productive *overall*.

In this case, task-merging means finding two different things that you're doing each day or week and blending them into a single task, thereby redeeming some time. You may not have a net gain of removing one task entirely, but the overall effect may save you time. Examples from some of our previous win assignments could be things like listening to the news on the commute to work instead of sitting on the toilet for 25 minutes in the morning scrolling news apps. It might mean migrating your forty minute weekly phone call with a local friend into a meet up at the gym as you were already going to be working out for an hour there anyway and they've been wanting to get back in shape. Spend time with your kids by having them help in the kitchen with simple dinner prep (bonus that they learn to cook). Be creative and look for ways to *merge tasks*.

| SUNDAY

Win: In Bed by 11pm

Repeat: Daily

I don't know if this is super scientifically supported but I have found it to be true as a rule of thumb that every hour of sleep prior to midnight is worth double in terms of rest.

Again, it seems like that's probably not true in a strict sense, but somewhere in there is a kernel of truth and we're going to use it. If you can actually be asleep by 11pm each night and count that hour as double, waking up an hour earlier than you normally would, still feeling refreshed, then you're saving seven hours a week!

This won't work for everyone as everyone's body and brain are different, but it's nearly a given that staying up *past* midnight doesn't bode well for your morning and your ability to master your morning as you've learned in week one.

BONUS: If that doesn't work, the other way (again, no science on this but still) is to incorporate more aggressive exercise into your day. Rule of thumb is an hour working out is an hour less of sleep needed, so not necessarily gained time but certainly gained productive energy.

In bed by 11pm.

Electricity is really just organized lightning.

- George Carlin

Week 3

Getting Organized

YOU'VE CLEARED OUT ALL of the time-wasting variables, you're still crushing your mornings, you've got new time & energy to invest in being more productive, nice job!

Now we're going to get *organized* so that you don't waste any of that momentum on pointless busywork.

| MONDAY

Win: Use a Calendar

Repeat: Daily

Most of you probably already have a calendar, so perhaps this isn't so much "get a calendar" as "actually start using the calendar you have" or perhaps "be smarter about how you use it" or even "stop using a paper calendar and move your stuff online." Wherever you're at on that scale, make the choice to up your game. Everyone should have a digital calendar. Not only is it faster and more accurate than transcribing all of your regular meetings by hand, you can (and should!) set reminder notifications for your key meetings and events. I prefer to get a notification the evening before (helps me remember what tomorrow brings) and then again 10 minutes prior for all of my key calendar items.

Share your calendar with family members so that you can see each other's events and schedules as well to more easily coordinate and maximize your time. Don't write in everything you're doing during the day, that's for task management software (we'll get to that) but do write in anything that takes you out of the house, any meetings or calls, and anything else unusual. It's also a good idea to note large bill due dates, tax filings, etc.

Use a calendar.

| TUESDAY

Win: Use Task Management Software

Repeat: Daily

If you did nothing else suggested in this book except for this one thing, you'd get like 80% of the productivity benefits. Taking time to write down what you need / want to do for the day and then marking things off as you accomplish them is HUGE. There are a zillion apps for this, I prefer "Trello" (it's simple and free) but there are others that offer different user interfaces and features. The key thing is to <u>find what works for you</u> and then <u>use it daily and forever</u>. Each morning (or even the night before) write down as individual tasks every major thing you already have in your calendar for that day, meetings, etc. Then write in everything else that you need / want to accomplish in terms of tasks & projects. Finally, check your email for new assigned tasks and add those in as well. Sort all of that pile into an order that makes sense for your day. Once you're into your work day, begin cranking through the list, marking things as "complete" as you finish them. Add new items as they come into your awareness via email / meetings. Re-sort and even migrate items to tomorrow or future days if necessary. Don't overfill your day, and don't lose what's important in the midst of what feels urgent.

Use task management software.

| WEDNESDAY

Win: Use File Folders

Repeat: As-Needed

For everything that you can't digitize or otherwise requires that you keep a physical paper copy, you need to start a filing system. Huge amounts of time are often wasted in looking for missing pieces of paper. Also piles of unsorted / unorganized paper can be a massive emotional drag to have around. Like an unmade bed, it alters your posture towards your work. If you haven't already, invest in a small portable file box (or even a freestanding two-drawer file) and a bunch of file folders. Sort out your current mess of papers and decide on some broad categories (taxes, utilities, credit card statements, car stuff, important receipts, etc.) and actually <u>label</u> your file folders and <u>note the year</u>. You'll want to recreate these file folders each January to keep your years separate for easy searching in the future. You're required to keep certain tax and financial documents for at least three years (and more in some cases, know your local laws) so those can be handy to keep within reach, like if you want to refinance your mortgage. Otherwise put older years into stackable boxes to keep in the attic or somewhere safe from water damage. Already have a filing system set up? Use it!

Use file folders.

| THURSDAY

Win: Set Up a Password System

Repeat: As Needed

Another common time-suck is trying to remember all your passwords. As a workaround, some folks just use the same password for everything (but having your accounts hacked also is a time-suck so don't do that) or making them up on the fly and promptly forgetting them, only to discover later that their browser has also forgotten them, etc. How many passwords do you have? Fifty? As a family, a hundred?

Save time and be more secure by developing a coded system. Pick letters, numbers, and / or symbols to represent common parts of password phrases you use. Put those reference hints into a spreadsheet that you can use to look up your answers, and then always use your system and always take note of new passwords as you create them.

If you can't remember what your hints refer to then keep a hardcopy at home in a secure place for reference.

You can share this spreadsheet with family members because it's also a common issue to have to troubleshoot family members who have forgotten their passwords and want help.

Set up a password system.

| FRIDAY

Hack: Everything with a Place, Everything in its Place

Repeat: As Necessary

Let's face it, you don't just lose paper, you're capable of losing just about anything. Some of this comes down to personality but in reality it's just a matter of actually having some kind of system for keeping track of your stuff. The basic way to not lose stuff is to have a "place" for everything in your life, and then to always seek to put those items back into that same place. Most folks have a certain spot in their kitchen where they keep their cups. And that's true for lots of stuff, but usually there is some line in the sand somewhere in your home where certain stuff doesn't really have an assigned place. They might have a spot out in the open where you might "often see it there" but then when it's *not* there it's hard to know where to begin to look. Perhaps different family members have different ideas about where that item goes, etc. The solution to this is that, as much as possible, select a spot that makes sense, that everyone is aware of, and agrees with, and that is willing to (try) to remember to put it back there right away after use. This will save countless minutes and even hours of searching for keys, coats, hats, books, AirPods, and chargers.

Everything with a place, everything in its place.

| SATURDAY

Hack: Schedule a Junk-Drawer Day

Repeat: Bi-Weekly (or As-Needed)

You know that stuff that you're supposed to do / find / repair / research / order or otherwise deal with that just never gets done? Important stuff like mailing your passport application in or researching pictures online to try and figure out what's going on with that rash?...all that stuff weighs on you as a never ending list and sometimes doesn't get tackled simply because it all seems too overwhelming. The way through this is two-fold: First, have a running list of junk-drawer tasks that you just aren't able to get to during the week, and put those into your task-management app as you think of them. Have them in a separate list you <u>can't see</u> so you're not stressed about them when you can't do anything about them. Secondly, calendar in a day every other week (Saturdays?) to focus solely on knocking one or two or more of these items off your list. Give yourself permission to ignore your normal lists that rule your life mid-week. This can also be a huge catharsis, to work on something "different" than what you normally deal with. Involve family members in these tasks if practical. Kids are great at holding flashlights when you're looking for the source of a water leak or under your car.

Schedule a junk-drawer day.

| SUNDAY

Hack: Boost Your Energy with Social Reinforcement

Repeat: *After* Successful Wins

By now you should be crushing more than just your mornings. You've mastered your mornings, cut back on time wasters, and now you're super organized with your calendar and your task management and your filing system and putting things where they go and even all that junk-drawer stuff is finally sorted and getting tackled one-by-one. You're feeling good.

But what? You're not feeling good? Some folks get to this point and are feeling drained. This probably means you're extroverted and this has all been very lonely, boring, not-exciting work. Time to bring social media into this! I know, I know, it might be a terrible temptation to waste time, but you've been good, you get a cookie. Social reinforcement & accountability are huge motivators. Boost your organizing energy by posting about your journey toward being more productive & organized. The positive reinforcement you get should help keep you going as we push deeper into harder stuff. **WARNING:** Do NOT share about ANYTHING you haven't yet done or accomplished. You will get all of the reward (undeservedly) ahead of time and not receive any new energy. Instead look forward to sharing, and use that energy to push through!

Boost your energy with social reinforcement.

Setting goals is the first step in turning the invisible into the visible.

- Tony Robbins

Week 4

Setting Goals

NOW YOU'RE MOVING...BUT WHERE are you going?

This week we're going to spend time clarifying your goals.

| MONDAY

Step: Brain-Dump all of your Existing Goals

Repeat: Once a Year (or As Needed)

This whole week we're going to focus on goal-setting. You might wonder why we didn't do this sooner but the reality is there is little point in setting goals if you don't have the tools, habits, and hacks to make them happen. Now that you're a bit more functional, we're going to start setting some near-term and long-term goals.

Also this is not a one-day-win kind of process, it's going to take all week to finish this, so instead of wins we're going to focus on "steps."

Today the step you're going to take is to grab a coffee or tea and a paper and pen and spend an hour or so writing down every single goal, spoken or unspoken, you have for your life. (Don't do this with anyone else, though if you have a life partner you might want to ask them to do this process also, but be on your own for now). These could be long term goals or short term goals, don't worry about their quality or nature, just dump it all out on the page and then tuck it away in a safe space. We'll come back to it tomorrow.

That's it. Go back to your normal day.

| TUESDAY

Step: Organize Your Goals

Repeat: Once a Year (or As Needed)

Grab a fresh cup of coffee or tea and pull that list back out. Add in any additional items that surfaced after a night of sleep, and then, on a new piece of paper begin grouping them into different categories. These could be subjects like:

School / Continuing Education / Degrees / Certifications

Work / Career / Financial / Saving / Investing

Relationships / Marriage / Parenting / Legacy

Physical / Health / Sports

Mental / Spiritual / Philanthropic / Social

You get the idea. Group them in whatever way that makes sense to you. And actually rewrite them out <u>by hand</u> again. Then grab a third page of paper and rework the list a third time, splitting each grouping into two piles: <u>near-term</u> and <u>long-term</u> goals. The end result should be a sort of grid with two columns (near and long term goals) and many rows, grouped by subject.

That's it for today, put the pages away in a safe place.

| WEDNESDAY

Step: Brainstorm Missing Goals

Repeat: Once a Year (or As Needed)

Pull that third page out again and look it over. After another night's sleep you probably have new ideas. Write those in.

You might also have totally new categories that you didn't realize you had goals for. Fill those into your existing page also if there's room. If not, rewrite it by hand again.

(You'll note that you're writing this and rewriting this out by hand several times, this is by design. The more you read / write / see these goals, the clearer they will become in your mind and the more likely that you'll be able to reach them.)

Now start to think outside the box. What kinds of goals are you obviously ignoring? Do you have a plan for retirement? Are you exercising regularly? Did you want to lose weight? Gain strength? Finish that great American novel you've never really started? What if you knew that you couldn't fail, what would you try? Are any of your existing goals incompatible with one another?

Finish up and put your latest page away in a safe place.

| THURSDAY

Step: Share Your Goals

Repeat: Once a Year (or As Needed)

This step is going to have the most relevance for those who are married or have some kind of life partner, though few people live in a complete social vacuum so even if you're single at this moment, there are probably other folks you can involve in this process. I'll describe each differently.

NOT SINGLE - If you haven't already, invite your life-partner to go through the prior steps, and then when you've both arrived at this part, sit down and compare notes. Hopefully there is already a significant amount of overlap and few surprises, but talk through those areas as they come up. Work to find shared goals in shared areas of life and then speak with wisdom and gentleness areas where there is less overlap. Revise as needed and sleep on the net results.

SINGLE - Find a parent, roommate, or close friend to share your life goals with. Ask for feedback and input and be willing to receive it with humility and grace (it's not easy to allow folks to speak into your life in this way, it can be scary and even frustrating). Take their input with a grain of salt, and revise your page as needed. Sleep on it.

| FRIDAY

Step: Identify & Refine Your "Goal Pathways"

Repeat: Once a Year (or As Needed)

This next step is a bigger job than can be done all at once, so pick just one or two areas of your goals and put them onto a new piece of paper. Don't do more than four or five goals and not from more than one or two areas. If one near-term goal seems to fit into the pathway of a long-term goal, nest it under that longer term goal as a "step along the way."

Start with the end in mind and then work your way backward to today, asking these questions: What does it look like, exactly, for me to accomplish this goal? What are the tangible, real-life steps that are required for me to get there?

This comes back to brainstorming and visualization, so just put everything down you can think of and then organize it after, reorganizing and rewriting it as often as necessary as you refine your "goal pathways." If your goal is a certification in a field, think through the requirements (passing a test) and the implied pathway steps (buying books, studying, taking practice tests online, paying a fee to sit for the real test, etc.). Near term could be researching what is required, and finding a testing center, etc. Work out a pathway for a few goals and then stop when you're feeling done or out of time.

| SATURDAY

Step: Identify & Refine Your "Goal Pathways" (Continued)

Repeat: Once a Year (or As Needed)

Pick up where you left off yesterday, adding in any new thoughts / ideas for the goals you focused on yesterday that have come to mind after a night's sleep.

Now pick a few additional goals to tackle and work through, using the same process again. Another example could be health related, such as losing weight. This could involve dietary research and experimentation, locating sources of food and supplements, finding a safe running route or buying weights for use at home, saving up for a smartwatch or registering for spin classes at a local gym, a visit to the doctor, a smart scale, or even buying books. Think of everything and put it into a pathway.

You may or may not finish identifying and refining pathways for all of your goals in just two days, but keep at it until you have clarity about your life and what you want to do. <u>The sure-fire way of not attaining your goals is to not identify them in the first place</u>. Having clear goals and pathways will begin to impact your daily choices. It's a slow process, embrace the slowness.

Rome wasn't built in a day and your life won't be either.

| SUNDAY

Step: Integrate Your Goals into Your Daily Life

Repeat: Daily

Now you have goals, and a pretty good idea of how you might get to accomplishing them. Today we're going to work to integrate the steps you've identified in your goal pathways into your daily life systems. This is going to be in two primary ways:

First, make sure you have your goals written out visually somewhere where you can see them and be reminded of them on a daily basis. This is incredibly important.

Second, as steps along your goal pathways naturally fit into your calendar and task management software, add them in. As you get better at this, more and more of your daily tasks will / should come into alignment under one or more of your goals.

Take it slow, this is a particularly difficult thing to do. Most folks experience blocks at this stage. It's fun to imagine goals. Pathways are a little trickier to put together. But then actually putting those into action can feel bad at first, like doing pull-ups or math homework.

Go slow, push through. It gets easier.

If we do not create and control our environment, our environment creates and controls us.

- Marshall Goldsmith

Week 5

Setting Limits

As YOU PICK UP speed, it's important to have guardrails to keep you from veering off the road.

This week we're going to focus on setting limitations that will help keep you on track.

| MONDAY

Hack: Set Working Hours

Repeat: Daily

Every day should have clearly defined work times and non-work times. The reason for this is that you can give yourself permission to restfully waste time online or read a book or go for a walk if you know you're not supposed to be working. Conversely, you can and should be strict with yourself (and those around you) when you're supposed to be working. I don't know how true or accurate this is, but I've heard that in office situations, most workers only average about two hours a day of actual work on projects. Part of this is probably due to going to meetings and reading email and them not counting those hours, but also factored in this is water cooler time, checking social media, filling out TPS reports, spacing out at your desk, etc., it happens.

Set clearly in your mind when you're supposed to be working and develop the discipline to be doing just that. Even if you're feeling unable to accomplish what you want, make it a rule that you have to actually sit at your desk or wherever, even if you're not actively working. Writers do this even if they are blocked from writing. Make yourself be there to work.

Set working hours.

| TUESDAY

Hack: Apply the 80/20 Principle

Repeat: As Needed

One of the ways you can achieve goals in shorter time-frames is to learn the 80/20 principle.[1] I covered this at-length in Scary Fast so I won't completely rehash it here, but the gist of it is that you get 80% of the results out of the first 20% of your effort, and that working through the final 20% is where 80% of the effort goes. Not all projects require 100% perfection, and so if you can safely scale back to anywhere between 80-90% perfection, you can complete projects in less than half the time and thereby complete twice as many projects. This rule has to be applied with wisdom and common sense, not all areas of life can be 80/20'ed, but many, many can.

Review your projects and goal pathways and consider where you're putting in too much time being a perfectionist and where rapidly getting things to 80-90% will suffice and allow you to move on to the next step or something new. These may also be goals that you identified last week as potentially having shorter time-frames and self-imposed due dates. And you'll get better at applying this over time, don't rush it. Apply the 80/20 principle.

---

1. Check out "The 80/20 Principle" by Richard Koch

| WEDNESDAY

Hack: Set Duration Limits

Repeat: As Needed

If you haven't yet read the original Scary Fast book there are several chapter that talk about this, but for now a quick summary: this thing called Parkinson's Law states that "stuff takes at least as long as you plan for it to take." The takeaway for us is that you need to get your calendar out and review some things. First, look at all of your projects. Projects can be related to school, work, or even some of the goals you hammered out last week. I'm sure they're all really, really great goals, and that the pathways you've worked out for them are realistic. However, for SOME of these projects / goals, you've probably given yourself way too much time to accomplish or finish them. Take some time today to review which projects or "pathway steps" you might move up the due date on. I recommend this especially if there are "real" due dates assigned to any of these, that you set a self-imposed due date that is at least a <u>week</u> in advance. This should still give you a very reasonable timeframe to finish or accomplish these projects but also buffer you against the unknown. This also forces out hidden time-wasting that gets baked in with distance goals or due dates.

Set duration limits.

| THURSDAY

Hack: Set Failure Metrics for Projects

Repeat: As Needed

Not all projects are going to be a win, and in a world where for every success you've got to press through five to seven failures, you'll never make progress toward that eventual win if you don't acknowledge your failures and move on. More than "cutting your losses," this is an opportunity to take what you've learned from a failed project and redirect that wisdom and energy into the *next* thing. Remember that success is largely the ability to move from failure to failure without loss of enthusiasm (first said by Churchill or Lincoln, no one is sure). But to do so you've actually got to *acknowledge the failure*, and you're more likely to do so in a timely manner if you have some idea of what failure looks like ahead of time. What you don't want to be is the person who has invested twenty years in the same failed idea and is so deep that they can't ever quit or their whole lives feel like a failure.

To fail well and to fail quickly, have a clear metric for what success looks like, but also a clear metric for what failure looks like as well. That way you know when you've crossed that line that says you've spent enough time, energy, money on XYZ and it's time to move on.

Set failure metrics for projects.

| FRIDAY

Hack: Practice Strategic Ignorance

Repeat: As Needed

Strategic Ignorance is the idea that you keep yourself intentionally unaware of certain levels of information that might otherwise distract you from being able to focus on the details that matter. Henry Ford was famous for this. He had other guys who could tell him the answers to questions when he needed them, but otherwise kept himself ignorant so he could focus on the big picture or on a particularly difficult problem that needed his full attention to fix.

In the same way, you can OVER research for a project and take on too much information, freezing yourself with inaction. Or you can spread yourself too thin trying to be "aware" or "in" on everything, and never focusing deeply on what you're supposed to be doing. If you have a life partner, it's likely you already do this to some degree, perhaps without realizing it. Each of you have areas that you tackle or take the lead on, such as hospitality or food prep or the finances, allowing the other to lead & excel in their own areas. This is taking that same principle but applying it more intentionally in the midst of your projects.

Practice strategic ignorance.

| SATURDAY

Hack: Limit Project Inputs

Repeat: As Needed

At first glance this may appear similar to the strategic ignorance hack we looked at yesterday, but it's slightly different. In this case you're not limiting *information* so much as *inputs*. This most often works out as who you're listening to and allowing to speak into your projects or life. If you're hearing from too many different people, and hearing too many different contradictory things, it can lead to fear and inaction.

Rather, develop a few close, safe relationships who have permission to speak into your life. And on projects, limit the number of people involved so that you don't end up with a product that is "designed by committee" or that dies due to there being "too many cooks in the kitchen." Getting the right three or four people in the room is often far better than five or seven, and then you can always take the project to a larger group for review and input, but further along in the process. This can function for your personal projects but also as you spend more and more time working with teams, both as a part of a team and as a team lead. Also limit the types / number of emails you're subscribed to, things you watch / read, etc.

Limit project inputs.

| SUNDAY

Hack: Learn to Say "No"

Repeat: As Needed

One of the dangers of becoming a more productive person is that with all of your saved time and extra "accomplishing" energy, you'll find more and more projects being offered to you, and you'll think you can do them all.

You can't do them all.

Ergo the final limitation you need to consider (or perhaps the first) is how and when you should say "yes" to a new project. All of the productivity hacks in the world won't help you be productive on something if you've got too many things going on at once. Yet so many people have trouble saying "no" that they end up saying "yes" to almost everything. Remember that every time you say "yes" to something you're saying "no" to something else. I literally never say "yes" to anything on the same day it's offered. I always say I'll think about it / sleep on it and get back to them in the next day or two with my answer. That helps relieve the momentary tension, and models good decision making. If it is such an urgent thing that they need an answer in that moment, then I probably have to say "no" as I'm not wanting to be a part of that which would compromise my existing commitments.

Learn to say no.

The greater the obstacle, the more glory in overcoming it.

- Moliere

Week 6

Overcoming Blocks

LIKE A FIGHTER JET, once you get going fast enough you're likely to run into productivity "sound barriers". But rather than always punching through them with a sonic boom, sometimes you're getting stuck.

This week we're going to work on overcoming blocks.

| MONDAY

Step: Identify Your Blocks

Repeat: As-Needed

We're over halfway! Perhaps it's felt like a long five weeks. At this point you might feel like you're starting to hit a wall. I've been pushing you pretty hard to make a lot of life changes, and change-fatigue is normal.

You've also probably discovered a number of things about yourself that you don't like, such as self-limiting beliefs, blocks, and other points of failure.

Our simple task for today is to make note of these blocks. What is it you're finding yourself stuck on at this point? Goal setting? Using the calendar? Task-management? What is it that you keep avoiding and finding yourself being super productive doing OTHER things just to avoid this one thing?

List all of them out on a piece of paper (or type them up if that's easier, writing these out by hand isn't important). Try and be a bit ruthless with yourself, these blocks will hide. Self-limiting beliefs are hard to see as we're often not loving them and don't want to look at them directly. Save your list in a safe place and / or set it aside for now.

| TUESDAY

Step: Confirm Your Blocks

Repeat: As-Needed

Get your list of blocks back out and add anything new that has become clear to you after a night's sleep.

Now do a super scary thing and ask your life partner (or whomever you shared your goals with) what kinds of things they think you're blocked on or areas of self-limiting beliefs. Don't show them what you already have, let them work with an open mind.

Make note of their contributions, without getting emotional or reacting. Writing them down doesn't make them true or mean you agree with them, just get them onto paper.

Next, give them your list and have them confirm or question each of those you have already identified.

Thank them for their time & input and humbly consider their suggestions. Receive what you find true and valuable and add it to your list.

Save / set it aside for now and go back to your normal day.

| WEDNESDAY

Step: Attack Your Blocks

Repeat: As-Needed

Now that you have a pretty good idea of your blocks, look them square in the face and allow yourself to be conscious of them. Don't look away. Then identify one that you would like to target for attack. (Over the rest of this week we'll cover hacks that can increase your attack-power for this exercise so don't worry if it feels too hard.) Clearly define what it looks like to overcome this blockage. It might not be "write a whole book" but simply, "start the first chapter". Or if your block is about cleaning out the fridge, it might just be "throw away all of the expired leftovers and food".

Once you've picked a blockage and what it looks like to overcome it, I want you to clear out a chunk of time to focus on it. Could be just an hour, or could be a half day, depending on the thing you are blocked on and what overcoming that block looks like in terms of time-spent. And then as they say over at Nike, "JUST DO IT." Practice ripping the bandaid off. See how it feels. Be curious to know what it feels like to overcome, and then ride that feeling. Usually the first few minutes are the hardest, then it gets easier and easier.

Attack your blocks.

| THURSDAY

Hack: Overcome Blocks with Resistance Training

Repeat: Weekly

One of the most powerful ways to increase your ability to overcome blockages is through resistance training, otherwise known as living weights or weight training. ***I have to put a disclaimer here because this is a very dangerous activity: It's easy to hurt yourself and many people shouldn't do this due to health conditions, consult your doctor, etc.** Having said that, most people SHOULD be lifting weights, not only for the health benefits but to radically alter their minds in terms of pressing through pain points and increasing their sense of power. Lifting a heavy weight teaches your brain that you can do hard things, things that seem too heavy to deal with. It's a priceless neurological hack and pays huge dividends. It also releases testosterone into your system which, as mentioned before, is basically the "get stuff done" hormone. It also reduces indices of depression and other moods that get in the way of productivity. Again, how you get into this I have to leave up to you. I would recommend trying out a local gym or Crossfit or something to get training on how to safely lift weights. From there you eventually could do it at home, etc. Find what works for you and start training.

Overcome blocks with resistance training.

| FRIDAY

Hack: Overcome Blocks with Cold Exposure

Repeat: Daily

Another very powerful way to train your body and your mind is cold exposure. These are ice baths and cold showers. ***Again, this is very, very dangerous to do, as you can black out and drown and / or fall over and hit your head and die. So I mention this with the very greatest trepidation that someone could get hurt trying this, and have to say that you're best to be sitting in a cold shower and that you never do an ice bath unsupervised (wear swim trunks and have someone monitoring you).**

The thirty seconds of cool water at the end of your shower have been training you for this exercise, and you should be ready to tackle it if you are able to put the proper safety measures into place. Some folks are more likely to lose consciousness than others so even if you find you don't have an issue, don't recommend this to others without the proper cautions.

All that said, again, very powerful for altering your body's chemistry, almost a reset of your nervous system and release of a lot of helpful chemicals for getting stuff done.

Overcome blocks with cold exposure.

| SATURDAY

Hack: Overcome Blocks by Breaking Conventions

Repeat: As-Needed

This is much safer than the previous two hacks, as long as what you attempt isn't illegal or something. The idea here is that you train your mind to overcome barriers by physically breaking social norms rules.[1] The classic example of this is to lie down on the floor in a public space for a few moments (e.g., Starbucks), but you could do anything that you find hard to do, such as speak to a stranger or sing in public, etc. Find something hard to do but that is still doable, and then step it up from there.

Alternatively you could tackle this in a more structured way by taking a public speaking course (.e.g, Toast Masters) or any other kind of hobby or training that you find difficult or scary: rock climbing, martial arts, skydiving, anything to push your limits. You don't have to do all of the above, just pick one thing. (Though mixing skydiving with martial arts sounds vaguely amazing...) As a result, you'll find that your ability to overcome your personal blocks will greatly increase as you overcome social ones.

Overcome blocks by breaking conventions.

---

1. See the TED Talk by Tim Ferriss: tim.blog/fear-setting

| SUNDAY

Step: Overcome Blocks with Self-Deception

Repeat: As Needed

When all else fails, just lie to yourself. There's a whole section on this in "Scary Fast" but the gist of it is that you can often overcome a block simply by telling yourself that you don't have to overcome it, but maybe "just take a quick look at the project." And that maybe you'll just grab a few links as resources for the research you'll have to do later, or pick up just a few toys on the ground, but you're not going to clean the whole living room. And maybe you don't, but once you're into it, maybe you also fold those clothes, and maybe you sweep up a bit, and maybe you end up cleaning the whole room.

You can quit any time, because you're not really there to do the job, but it doesn't hurt to get a head start, your future self will find it easier if the job is already rolling. But once you're rolling...it's easier to keep going than to stop.

Lie to yourself and see where you end up.

Overcome blocks with self-deception.

It is not how much we have, but how much we enjoy, that makes happiness.

- Charles Spurgeon

Week 7

Happiness Hacks

SIX WEEKS IN AND you're back on the couch, hugging a bag of chips. Why?

Sadness happens.

Happy people are productive people, so this week we're going to review the seven hacks that result in (average) human happiness. As you grow in these you should see a correlation in your ability to follow through on what we've covered so far.

| MONDAY

Hack: Work First, Play Later

Repeat: Daily

I believe 50% of human happiness boils down to rightly ordering work & play. Spending your morning playing video games and eating Lucky Charms might be awesome, but if you have a project due the next day, that's on the back of your mind the whole time, poisoning the enjoyment of your leisure activities. And then when it finally comes time to "knuckle down" and get to work, it's really depressing, and sometimes you find that you didn't even leave yourself enough time and are up late or fail to finish.

Alternatively, getting up and getting started right away allows you to crush your work ahead of your play, and then when you rest, you can truly rest, doubly happy in that you're not burdened by that "thing" that's due, and instead basking in that warm feeling of accomplishment.

It's the same amount of work & play in any given day, but rightly ordered, radically changes how you FEEL during that same day.

Work first, play later.

| TUESDAY

Hack: Tidy Up Your Workspace

Repeat: As Needed

Part of the reason we have you start this whole process with making your bed isn't just to start you off with a productivity win but because it also makes you happy (and conversely a messy, undone bed makes you unhappy). This same principle applies to your workspace. If you arrive at your workspace (at home or at the office) and you're immediately confronted with piles of unsorted paperwork, dirty coffee cups, and crumbs on the floor, you're psychologically weighted with a mass of unfinished "cleanup" work. This makes you sad and stressed, before you're even into your *actual* work.

Instead make an effort to create an organized and emotionally positive space for yourself. When you first go to your office space today, pause at the entry and take it all in. Pay attention to your gut. How does your work space make you feel? What are the trouble-spots or eye-sores? If you could snap your fingers and change anything about your workspace, what would it be? In some cases you may realize that you actually need to find a new workspace entirely, to get a fresh start. But in most cases simply cleaning up (file those papers, reduce clutter) will make a big difference.

Tidy up your workspace.

| WEDNESDAY

Hack: Let There Be Light

Repeat: As Needed

You need light to be happy, but life has so many ways of keeping you in the dark. Perhaps your workspace doesn't have a window or skylight, poor lighting fixtures, or perhaps you live in a part of the world with dark winter months. The first step to bringing more light into your workspace is figuring out why it's so dark.

Sunlight is best, so if you have a window, make the most of it. Get it uncovered. If privacy is an issue, use a sheer shade or blind, or get a fixture that lowers from the top. Reorient your desk so you're getting the right amount of light into your eyes. Or perhaps move your desk to a new room / office (if you have that option). Maybe it means trimming those bushes or a tree that's casting your space into deep shadow.

No natural light to be had? Improve your situation by removing fluorescent light bulbs and swapping for 3000K LED bulbs (this may also help prevent cancer, time will tell). But if that's all not enough, purchase a S.A.D. (seasonal affective disorder) light from Amazon. They're super bright so use it as-instructed, stepping yourself up in stages.

Let there be light.

| THURSDAY

Hack: Don't Work Too Much or Too Little

Repeat: Weekly

A few years back there was this study where they discovered that 33 hours was about the most optimal amount of work-week hours for happiness. Work less than 33 hours, sadness starts to creep in. Work more than 33 hours, happiness starts to go back down, sadness returns. Another more recent study showed better work results on a four-day work week than the traditional five-day week (no footnotes, sorry, just Google these ones).

Hyper-specific numbers aside, this feels true, doesn't it? Remember any unemployed, childless days, sitting at home at 10:00 AM, watching The Price is Right, punctuated by those ads for culinary & nursing schools? Depressing. Folks need stuff to do to be happy. But not too much stuff. Most of us don't have the pleasure of working just 33 hours a week, we're putting in at least 40, and that's OK. The takeaway of this principle is that going too far in either direction isn't a good thing, so going way *above* 40 is going to be hard on your system, especially all at one job. In terms of productivity, as you work longer hours, you'll be less happy, and therefore less and less productive. Do more in less time, but not more in more time. Don't work too much or too little.

| FRIDAY

Hack: Pay Yourself First

Repeat: Weekly

Being broke is stressful. You've probably heard this phrase before, "Pay yourself first." The idea is that rather than paying all of your bills and giving yourself whatever is left over, you should make yourself into your own creditor and pay yourself (save / invest) a small amount FIRST, before paying all of your other bills. This is mostly a mental trick and obviously you have to have something to spare, but start with whatever you can, $5 or $100 a week, and put it into an account to be invested in something safe (ETFs are a popular choice if you're not retiring any time soon). Do this forever. Even if you have credit card debt and student loans and a mortgage. Start putting stuff away bit by bit. You will find that having a growing pile of assets in the background of your life will radically alter your emotional posture.[1] You will also be saving for retirement. This is not financial advice but I would recommend starting doing this as soon as you're legally able (18 usually) and then don't move stuff around too much. Obviously consult with your tax professional / accountant / investment guy (but don't get suckered into a mutual fund). Pay yourself first.

---

1. Check out "The Richest Man in Babylon" by George S. Clason

| SATURDAY

Hack: Exercise

Repeat: As Needed

YOU: "Hey! You said no running was required for this process, and I've already been told to 'move my body' AND to lift weights, what more do you want??"

Do you want to be happy?

YOU: "…….yes."

Well I'm not saying you have to start jogging or anything, but exercise is 100% going to make you happier. Lifting weights and going for a walk and stretching are great, but actually doing something that gets your heart rate up is going to release endorphins (happiness juice) and lower your biological age.

YOU: "Wait, I actually get younger the more I exercise??"

Sort of, biologically your tissues can "de-age" slightly, Google it. But do some cardio first.

Exercise.

| SUNDAY

Hack: Invest in Real-World Relationships

Repeat: As Needed

As more folks work from home and as Amazon delivers everything within days (if not hours), it's easier than ever to just never leave the house and never have to interact with people. And this is bad for your happiness, and therefore (eventually) bad for your productivity. You need to invest in real-world relationships.

YOU: "But what about my Metaverse friends?"

I'm glad you have those but to be truly happy as a human being you ALSO need real-world interactions with people. Brain science identifies face to face interactions as being the trigger for releasing the chemistry of joy.[2] Phone calls don't do it. Zoom calls don't even do it. You need to see their face, looking at your face, and approving of you. That's it. Plus going to see other humans in-person will force you to start putting on pants. Pants = Happiness. Yes I know, you gave up on getting dressed a while back, even though we talked about it. Going out will fix that. Invest in real-world relationships.

---

2. Check out "The Other Half of Church: Christian Community, Brain Science, and Overcoming Spiritual Stagnatio" by Jim Wilder & Michel Hendricks

Being aware of your fear is smart. Overcoming it is the mark of a successful person.

- Seth Godin

Week 8

Mastering Fear

WE'VE JUST SPENT A week developing your happiness. Now we're going to spend a week on mastering your *fears*.

This process is going to be very similar to the one we used to address your blocks. Blocks & fears are similar, but fears run much deeper and can be more destructive.

| MONDAY

Step: Identify Your Fears

Repeat: As Needed

Our task for today is to make note of your fears. What are you afraid of?

It's OK to start with the obvious: spiders, heights, public speaking. Get those all down on paper, but then dig deeper...what surfaces? You might have to talk-therapy yourself a bit out loud in your room, but ask the question and let stuff rise to the top. Failure, pain, rejection?

Success?

List all of them out on a piece of paper (or type them up if that's easier, writing these out by hand isn't important). Try to be a bit ruthless with yourself. Like blocks, fears will hide. Save your list in a safe place and / or set it aside for now.

| TUESDAY

Step: Confirm Your Fears

Repeat: As Needed

Get your list of fears back out and add anything new that has become clear to you after a night's sleep.

Now (again) do a super scary thing and ask your life partner (or whoever you shared your goals & blocks with) what kinds of things they think you're afraid of. Don't show them what you already have, let them work with an open mind.

Make note of their contributions, without getting emotional or reacting. Writing them down doesn't make them true or mean you agree with them, just get them onto paper.

Next, give them your list and have them confirm or question each of those you have already identified.

Thank them for their time & input and humbly consider their suggestions. Receive what you find true and valuable and add it to your list.

Save / set it aside for now and go back to your normal day.

| WEDNESDAY

Step: Visualize Fearlessness

Repeat: As Needed

Now that you have a pretty good idea of your fears, look them square in the face and allow yourself to be conscious of them. Don't look away.

Now start a new page and write out what life would look like if you didn't have each of these fears. This could get complex to visualize but find the low hanging fruit and start there:

1. I kill my own spiders, instead of asking for help.

2. I deeply enjoy the view from cliffs, balconies, and suspension bridges.

3. When suddenly asked to speak in front of a crowd, I need no prep time and enjoy the spotlight.

4. When my business suddenly doubles, I immediately know how to scale and deploy the new capital.

Etc., you get the idea. Keep at it until you have a picture of what a fearless life looks like for you. Then write them out on a fresh piece of paper or card and post it somewhere where you'll see it on a daily basis.

Visualize fearlessness.

| THURSDAY

Hack: Overcome Your Fears Through Exposure Therapy

Repeat: As Possible

You've identified your fears AND thought deeply about what it would look like to live without them. But fears don't just go away on their own. Processing through them requires work, and could end up involving some kind of counselling or therapy, depending on why they're there. None of what follows is medical advice, and if you're already seeing someone regarding mental health issues or for personal healing and growth, make sure to involve them in this process.

There are a few different ways to tackle fear, but the number one way is through exposure therapy. That's where you seek to (safely!) expose yourself to what you're afraid of. Again, safety is paramount, because you could end up making your fear worse if you decide to sit in a box of spiders or something. Instead, Google "Lucas the Spider" and watch these cute animated spider videos. Then watch videos of (real) jumping spiders (also pretty cute). Work your way up to watching the movie Arachnophobia (if you can get through that, you're probably cured).

Overcome your fears through exposure therapy.

| FRIDAY

Hack: Overcome Your Fears by Being Prepared

Repeat: As Needed

Fear of public speaking? Afraid you'll bomb the presentation? Sometimes that fear is simply the awareness that you're not really prepared to do what you're supposed to do. If you're supposed to give a speech and you haven't finished writing it, you should probably be a little uncomfortable. Conversely, overcoming our fears is often tied to being prepared for what comes. Thankfully, the skills you've been developing up to this point can help you be more prepared.

YOU: "What if what I'm afraid of shows up unexpectedly?"

Great question. This is where the Boy Scouts have life hacked with their motto "Always Be Prepared." Not that you have to become a "prepper" and dig a well in your backyard, but there *is* a confidence that comes from being "ready" for whatever you can think of. Go back to your list of fears. What, if anything, can you do to be prepared? Carry note cards for an impromptu speech? (People will think it *hilarious* that you have those, especially if you have BLANKS where you're supposed to verbally fill in the NAME / EVENT of whatever impromptu thing you have to speak at.) Get creative.

Overcome your fears by being prepared.

| SATURDAY

Hack: Overcome Your Fears as a Group

Repeat: As Needed

Exposure and preparedness not cutting it for some of your fears? Humans are social creatures and there are net-benefits to tackling problems as a group. Get with others who share your fear and talk through everything: Where you think the fear originates, any fears "behind the fear" that are more of the real issue, maybe how you have tried and been unable to overcome this fear, etc.

Then listen to others share. Perhaps insights they've had will help you. If there are people who don't share the fear but are there to be supportive, let them speak into your life. Take what they say with a grain of salt, but listen humbly and try not to take offense. There can be much wisdom found, even from our enemies or those who wish us ill. They can sometimes be the truest voices in our lives.

But ideally you're with supportive people who can empathize and allow you to get outside your own head on this issue. This is essentially self-organized "group therapy." Don't go it alone.

Overcome your fears as a group.

| SUNDAY

Step: Overcome Your Fear with the Help of a Professional

Repeat: As Needed

So you've already tried "exposure therapy" and "group therapy" and you're still struggling? You've maybe bootstrapped yourself as far as you're going to get on this on your own. It could be time to speak to an actual therapist.

YOU: "I don't need to see a therapist."

Oh sure, it doesn't have to be a therapist specifically. It could be connecting with a life coach, consultant, counselor, or even a pastor in a church, whatever you feel most comfortable with. The point is that there is value in connecting with someone who has formal *experience* and *training* in the area that you're struggling with.

Whether you pay for it or get it free, getting guidance from someone who knows what they're doing sometimes is the only path out of the forest. Don't let social stigma or your own pride get in the way of overcoming a limiting fear.

Overcome your fear with the help of a professional.

There's no such thing as work-life balance. There are work-life choices, and you make them, and they have consequences.

- Jack Welch

Week 9

Finding Balance

BY NOW YOU SHOULD be really moving. Maybe not *Scary* Fast but still, getting *a lot* of stuff done.

This week's theme is going to be about finding balance in the midst of all this newfound productivity.

| MONDAY

Hack: Take a Break

Repeat: As Needed

Maybe after this you go on to read (or reread) the original Scary Fast book, and that's totally fine. But before you do, let's finish this final week together and learn how to balance everything out. And that starts with the opposite of getting something done: Taking a break.

Yes, if you've managed to get yourself into a "flow state" of high productivity then you don't want to wreck it by taking a break. Those are special, guard them. However under normal conditions you should be following this rule: Every 20 minutes, stand for 20 seconds, and look at something at least 20 feet away (20/20/20).

Maybe stretch a little, grab a sip of water. Doing that will both protect your body and keep you mind limber for productivity.

Note that this is NOT a time to check email or social media or anything else. Just a quick stand and stretch and then back at it. Longer breaks should be worked in every hour or two, in which case you might employ the other hacks discussed this week.

Take a break.

| TUESDAY

Hack: Go Outside

Repeat: As Needed

Taking a longer break? Go outside. Notice your breath. Often when we've been working for an hour or two we're holding our breath without realizing it. Release your diaphragm and breathe in deeply, taking in fresh air.

Studies have shown that being able to see a tree from where you live / work actually adds time onto your life.[1] Look at a tree, or better, walk in a forest of trees. The Japanese call this "forest bathing". It's a thing, and it's good for you.

Look at the sky. Not only is stuff in the sky at least 20 feet away (check) but also it helps give perspective to your problems (they're not that big).

And finally, if you're lucky, the sun will be out. Don't look at the sun directly but close your eyes and tilt your face to take in max vitamin D production for a few moments.

Go outside.

---

1. Source study: https://ehp.niehs.nih.gov/doi/10.1289/ehp.1510363

| WEDNESDAY

Hack: Move Your Body

Repeat: As Needed

You can do this inside or out (double points for out) but move your body. There is a very good chance that most of you reading this have "indoor" jobs that involve sitting. Our bodies were made for movement and are happiest when they've experienced a physical load. You're perhaps already getting some of that with lifting weights but any kind of movement is going to make a difference to your day. Easy ways to add this in are:

1. More pushups

2. Going for a walk

3. Longer period of stretching

4. Jazzercise (purely optional)

The main idea is to just get yourself moving. If you can hit any of your other goals for the day at the same time, such as calling your mom, great. Call her and talk on the phone while going for a walk.

Move your body.

| THURSDAY

Hack: Take a Power Nap

Repeat: As Needed

Sometimes your brain is just done, and no amount of stretching, walking, sunshine, or coffee is going to be enough. And that's OK. People are realizing that naps aren't just for babies. Big companies are installing napping pods in their common areas. If you work from home (thanks Zoom), this is easy. If you actually go somewhere to work and your boss hasn't created a napping location yet, maybe grab some nap-science data and do a cost-benefit analysis for them.

YOU: "Napping makes me groggy."

You're just doing it wrong. The trick is to not nap too long. Obviously you can set an alarm to wake yourself up after 15-25 minutes but other ways to keep yourself from going "too deep" are to drink a cup of coffee just prior to napping and / or nap in a place with a lot of ambient "people noise" (like the couch in the living room). And finally, don't pressure yourself to sleep. Just give yourself permission to "rest your eyes" for 20 minutes and often you'll find you've dozed for a bit. Gets easier as you get older. Amazing brain-reset.

Take a nap.

| FRIDAY

Hack: Flip Tasks

Repeat: As Needed

I talk at-length about "task switching" in the original Scary Fast book, where you trick yourself into thinking you're taking a break but you're really just "switching" to do a different task. Works great.

This is a similar but slightly more specific version that is directed not towards productivity but towards our theme of finding balance. What I'd like you to do in this case is *flip* between a physical and a non-physical task. Doing something mentally taxing? Flip to mowing the lawn or doing the dishes.

Doing something physically taxing? Flip to filing your taxes or answering emails.

Flipping between placing a load on your physical body and on your mental faculties allows each some recovery time. You're more limited in what you can accomplish than with straight "task switching" but it'll leave you feeling less burned by the end of the day. **EXAMPLE:** I'm writing this on Christmas Eve and as soon as I'm done I'm going to "flip" to assembling & wrapping some presents.

Flip tasks.

| SATURDAY

Hack: Chose a Cheat Day

Repeat: As Needed

Remember how on the very first Saturday I made you get dressed even though you didn't need to? And I promised that you could eventually stay in your pajamas on a Saturday? You've arrived! In fact what I would recommend is that one day a week you throw out all of these rules that you've worked so hard to follow.

YOU: "Really?"

Yep, you don't even have to floss today.

YOU: (tears in eyes) "I really hate flossing..."

I know.

But it's not a rest day, you're still supposed to be working and getting stuff done. Maybe today is your junk-drawer day we talked about. Or maybe you're going to get a bunch of exercise in or work on the yard, whatever. Just allow yourself to enjoy the work without seeking to maximize your productivity.

Choose a cheat day.

| SUNDAY

Hack: Practice a Sabbath Day

Repeat: Weekly

Notice how yesterday's "cheat day" *wasn't* a rest day, you were still supposed to be working? *Today* is your rest day. Even God rested on the seventh day so you probably should too. Doesn't have to be Sunday, can be whatever day works for you / for your family. Humans need a day off. From everything.[2]

Again, this is different from your cheat day where you're still working but not trying too hard to maximize your productivity by following all of the little wins and hacks and habits you've formed, etc. Today you <u>do</u> need to do all of your habits.

YOU: "What? Flossing is back?"

Yep. Because if you are *undisciplined* on your rest day, it's going to just become a self-indulgence day. That was your cheat day, where you were *productive* but *unstructured.*

Today you're *structured*, but supposed to be *unproductive,* at least in the traditional sense (you may still hit social goals by being with friends & family, etc.).

Practice a Sabbath day.

---

2. Check out "The Emotionally Healthy Leader" by Peter Scazzero

Conclusion

YOU DID IT! NINE weeks of making daily, incremental changes to your life. I hope that this book has lived up to its name and *assisted* in *launching* you off of the "couch" and into a posture of organized, goal-driven, productivity.

I also hope you have managed to find a happy balance between being productive and not burning out. If you are still struggling with stress or burnout, go back and work through the final chapter a second time. These changes don't always come easy, and being productive is not the same as being happy and at peace. You have to fight to learn both and do the work to allow them to co-exist.

If you want to go further and haven't yet read the original book in this series, that's a great next step. You can find "Scary Fast: 7 Advanced Hacks to Boost Your Productivity 1,000x" at ScaryFastBook.com, available in Print and for Kindle.

Note that the emphasis in that book is on **Advanced**.

Because believe it or not, you can go quite a bit faster yet...

ME: "Enjoy this book? Consider leaving a review!"

YOU: "I don't know…I'm pretty busy."

ME: "Don't you love being able to read reviews that help you make wise purchases on Amazon?"

YOU: "Well…yes."

ME: "Be that hero! Write a really great review and help someone else make a good decision."

YOU: "…"

ME: "Or any kind of review. Even a review of meager effort on your part."

YOU: "That sounds more doable. I just don't like all the pressure."

ME: "No problem. Anything is fine."

YOU: "Fine, I'll do it tomorrow."

ME: "What? Why not do it today?"

YOU: "Fine."

ME: "Why not do it right NOW?"

YOU: "FINE!"

YOU: (going to do review on Amazon…)

YOU: (coming back unsuccessful) "I can't find your book."

ME: "Easy, just go to BrianMichaelStegner.com and that'll take you right to my author page, and all of my books will be there."

YOU: "You have other books?"

ME: "Oh yes, but don't get distracted. Write that review first!"

Brian Michael Stegner (1979-) was born in Albany, New York, grew up in Portland, Oregon, and attended college in Chicago and Saskatchewan. Primarily a storyteller, Brian specializes in 'Dry-fi', a mashup of literary fiction, nonfiction, science fiction, and dry humor. When not writing, he divides his time between family, church planting, entrepreneurial ventures, coaching, and reluctantly traveling the world.

He lives in Montreal, Québec with his wife and kids.

www.ingramcontent.com/pod-product-compliance
Lightning Source LLC
Chambersburg PA
CBHW031439210526
45464CB00005B/2261